Davide Cali would like to thank:

Nicole, the intern, who did all of the iconographic research,
and then dreamt of chupacabras and sea serpents for months.

Giuliano, for his friendship, his advice and his scientific help.

Mari, who's afraid of reptiles and unknown creatures, but who
listened to me when I was talking to her about all the scary creatures
of this book.

My father and my mother, who, when I was a child, bought me
so many books about animals.

MONSTERS & LEGENDS

CYCLOPS, KRAKENS, MERMAIDS AND OTHER IMAGINARY CREATURES THAT REALLY EXISTED!

Written by Davide Cali

Illustrations by Gabriella Giandelli

 FLYING EYE BOOKS

TABLE OF CONTENTS

- 2 -

WERE OUR ANCESTORS MAD?

The folktales and legends told for centuries by our ancestors are filled with stories of monsters that modern science has shown to be little more than myth and superstition.
But if our forbears truly believed in the terrifying Kraken and beautiful Mermaids, if they honestly thought they could see Unicorns and the Cyclops, were they all mad?
It's tempting to say yes - who else but a madman would believe in fishtailed women, horned horses, one-eyed giants and humongous sea creatures with thousands of tentacles?

But our ancestors weren't mad at all. They were just ignorant. And very, very impressionable.

It may be true that these fantastic creatures never existed, but it's also true that they were more than just the mere inventions of our ancestors' imaginations. Sailors, fishermen, scientists and writers from the past really did see mysterious creatures lurking just out of plain sight...
But they were not quite what they thought they saw...

Curious yet? Read on!

ANIMAL GAMES

The ancient Greek philosopher Aristotle (384-322 BC) wrote the first thorough classification of the animal world. But it wasn't until the 18th century, thanks to the work of Carl Linnaeus, that animals were first identified in a precise and systematic way.

Before Carl Linnaeus, humans had only named a few of the planet's animals. People were frightened when they spotted an animal they didn't recognise, and their minds began to play tricks on them. They saw normal animals as supernatural beings with monstrous powers. To describe these strange, new creatures, people invented a game - when they discovered a new animal, they looked for similarities with creatures they already knew to try and describe it. When their imaginations ran wild, our ancestors created weird and mysterious new creatures out of animals that most of us are very familiar with today. Here are a few examples:

(If you read these descriptions carefully, it shouldn't be too hard to work out what these monsters really are!)

THE CAMELOPARD
This animal had a leopard's patches, a horse's neck, a cow's hoofs, and a camel's head. It first appeared in ancient Egyptian and Babylonian frescoes.

THE SEA PIG
Sailors from the 16th century were the first to mention this peculiar animal. It had a pig's head, a wild boar's tusks, a dragon's paws and a fish's tail. The species from the northern seas was reputed to be wild and ferocious but still not as dangerous as the one living in the southern oceans.

THE VEGETABLE LAMB OF TARTARY

This was a legendary plant from Central Asia. Sheep grew on its branches. It was also called Barometz (which means "lamb" in the local language). But did this tree ever exist?

THE CROCUTA CROCUTA

Described for the first time by Pliny the Elder (23 - 79 AD), the Crocuta crocuta was as fast as a wild donkey, with a lion's neck, tail and breast and the hooves of a cow. It had a smile that stretched from ear to ear and could even impersonate the human voice.

THE GULON

This creature, which roamed the Scandinavian woods, was said to be the size of a dog, with a cat's head, razor-sharp claws, long hair, a fox's tail and a huge appetite.

WHAT REAL ANIMALS DO YOU THINK COULD BE HIDING BEHIND THESE TALES?

WHAT WE KNOW:

The Sea Pig is nothing but a walrus. The fierce animal seen in the southern seas was a seal.

The Camelopard is actually a giraffe!

The Crocuta crocuta is a spotted hyena. For a long time, its laugh was mistaken for a human voice.

The Vegetable Lamb of Tartary turned out to be a cotton plant! The people from Tartary (known now as the Great Steppe) thought that this plant grew little lambs which, when set free from the tree, left their wool stuck in the branches. The fact that nobody ever saw an animal emerge from the tree never stopped anyone believing the story. It was the only way to make sense of this furry plant!

The Gulon is an animal living in the forests of Europe and North America: it's called the glutton because of its big appetite. You might recognize its other name: Wolverine - it inspired the famous character from the X-Men comics!

THE UNICORN'S MAGICAL HORN

The Unicorn is one of the best-known mythological creatures. Its legend began in Ancient Egypt where it was described as a white horse with a single long horn on its forehead. In the Middle Ages, the horn was thought to have magical powers, like the ability to cure poison. It is said that Pope Boniface VIII owned four of them – just to be safe. Unicorn horns were sold in town markets up until the 19th century. It wasn't until 1827 that the French naturalist Georges Cuvier, unable to prove that the Unicorn existed, suggested removing the creature from bestiaries.

SO WHERE DID THE HORNS THAT WERE SOLD IN TOWN MARKETS COME FROM?

WHAT WE KNOW:

Let's start with the horn: it's the only part of this animal that ever really existed. It was actually the tusk of an animal called the narwhal - a sea mammal, much like a dolphin - that lives in the Arctic Ocean. Fishermen from the north hunted narwhals for their valuable tusks.

AH!

And what about the animal itself? It is possible that the first people who described the Unicorn actually saw the oryx, which is a white antelope from Africa. Male oryxes have two horns but they often lose one while fighting amongst themselves – starting to sound familiar?

The narwhal's tusks had absolutely nothing in common with the oryx's horns but for medieval merchants there was a lot of money to be made by pretending that a narwhal tusk was the horn of the mythical unicorn. Perhaps it was no accident the myth survived!

CYCLOPS!

In Greek mythology, Cyclopes were mysterious one-eyed giants who knew the secrets of iron and forged Zeus' thunderbolts. In Homer's Odyssey, Ulysses met their descendants in Sicily. Having forgotten the skills of their ancestors, the Cyclopes had become simple shepherds. Well, maybe 'simple' doesn't quite cut it... they had become very large and very bloodthirsty shepherds.

BUT DID THE CYCLOPS REALLY EXIST?

WHAT WE KNOW:

The word Cyclops comes from the Ancient Greek word *kiklops* and means "circle-eyed". Amongst the barbarians who lived in Sicily before the Greeks colonized it, there was a tribe that the Greeks called the Cyclops.

But how was the myth of the one-eyed giant born?

Medieval archaeologists were astonished when they unearthed what they thought was the skeleton of Polyphemus, one of the Cyclopses that Ulysses met in Sicily. Even though the bones didn't match the skeleton of a giant human, for many years everyone believed that the skeleton of a Cyclops had really been found. It was only in the 18th century that scientists realised that what they'd uncovered was in fact the skeleton of a dwarf elephant.

The legend's roots probably lie in Sicily, where a species of dwarf elephants lived in the Stone Age. The discovery of these skeletons, and especially the cavity in their skull, convinced people that there truly had been one-eyed giants on the island. As they already knew that a tribe named Cyclops used to live in Sicily, they mixed both pieces of information and the myth of the Cyclops was born.

AN EASY MISTAKE TO MAKE

You don't have to be stupid to mistake elephant bones for a Cyclops skeleton. Think about it: it was much easier to believe that the bones belonged to giant human beings than strange creatures like elephants, which had never been seen before in Sicily.

ON THAT NOTE, DOES GIDEON MANTELL'S NAME RING A BELL? PROBABLY NOT...

WHAT WE KNOW:

In 1822, the British geologist Gideon Algernon Mantell discovered the bones of a large animal that looked at first glance like a mammal, perhaps a rhinoceros.

Years later, Mantell decided that the bones actually belonged to an unknown animal, with teeth that looked like those of an iguana. He called his new discovery Iguanodon. This realization was the first in a series that led to the discovery of a group of animals that had been extinct for millions of years: the dinosaurs.

But Mantell's first reconstruction of the Iguanodon wasn't correct: the geologist imagined a giant horn-nosed lizard that walked on four legs. It was only toward the end of the 19th century that the Iguanodon was correctly reconstructed on two legs and without a horn. What Mantell had thought was the horn finally found its place back where it should have been all along... as its thumb bone!

We shouldn't be too hard on Mantell - remember that he was a pioneer in a science that didn't yet exist. And recent studies have shown that the Iguanodon, as a marsh animal, could have walked on both two and four legs at different times!

HALF WOMAN, HALF FISH

Before we do anything else with the Mermaid, let's revise our history! In the Near East, the earliest tales describe creatures that were half bird, half woman. In ancient Greek mythology, such creatures were called Harpies. They had a very short fuse and were known for their ferocity. In fact, some people still use the word Harpy today to describe a woman with a terrible temper!

The image of the Mermaid changed over time, from half-woman, half-bird, she became half-woman, half-fish. Like the Cyclops, Mermaids are mentioned in the Odyssey. Their singing turned men mad, so Odysseus told his crew to stuff wax in their ears so they couldn't hear the Siren song. Sailors certainly love to make up stories, but from the time of Homer until the 18th century, they still believed that Mermaids were real.

WERE THESE FISHY VISIONS JUST THE PRODUCT
OF A SAILOR'S OVERACTIVE IMAGINATION?
NOT EXACTLY.

WHAT WE KNOW:

Sailors really did see something: a creature called the dugong, a kind of large marine mammal that used to be widespread in the Mediterranean Sea. The female dugong has teats that look very similar to a woman's. But aside from their teats, female dugongs look nothing like their human counterparts: so how could sailors ever take those blubbery mammals for fishtailed women?

A few things contributed to this misunderstanding. Firstly, sailors could never see the whole dugong, as most of their body stays in the water as they swim, so all that could be seen was a fishy tail and what looked like a woman's breasts. Add to that the fact that crews were often drunk (rum, being easier to preserve than

water, was the drink of choice on long sea voyages and provided a safe, if alcoholic, source of hydration) and you have a simple recipe:

Take one strange, ladylike sea creature with what looks like a fish tail, mix with a whole lot of rum and you get a mermaid.

BEWARE OF THE KRAKEN!

The Kraken is a gigantic legendary sea monster. Its name comes from the Norwegian word krake, meaning "a twisted or crooked animal". The origin of the Kraken myth goes back to the 13th century, but it's not until the 18th and 19th centuries that sailor stories about the Kraken really start multiplying! Stories were told of ships being attacked and destroyed by a creature with tentacles over a kilometre long. Carl Linnaeus (remember him?) mentioned the Kraken in his first book in 1735, under the scientific name of Microcosmus marinus, but it doesn't appear in his following books, as he couldn't prove its existence.

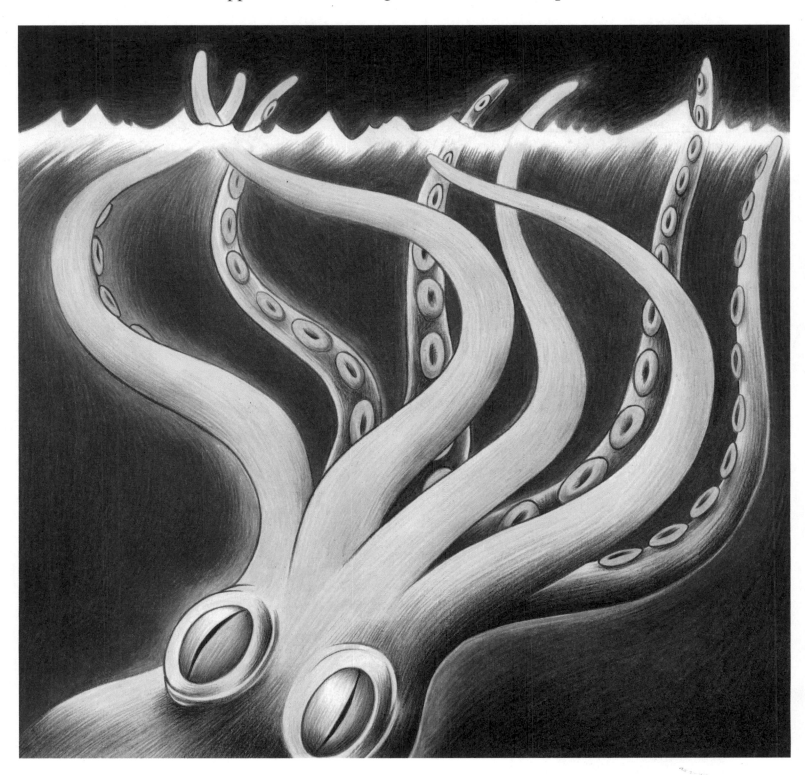

SO, DID THE KRAKEN EVER REALLY EXIST?

WHAT WE KNOW:

For a long time, zoologists have been studying a mysterious animal that lives at the very bottom of the ocean and only sometimes comes to the surface: the colossal squid.

The largest specimen to be found was almost 10 metres long, but it has been claimed that the creature can be as long as 25 metres and weigh up to 2 tons.

Colossal squid corpses have been found on beaches around the globe for the past four hundred years but few people have ever seen one alive.

In September 2004, a Japanese research team managed to film an 8 metre long giant squid swimming 900 meters beneath the waves.

It seems very likely that the Kraken was just a giant squid, or, as some claim, a shoal of giant squid. But as squid are solitary hunters people are still puzzled as to how or why they would have collected in large groups, so close to the surface... maybe something even more sinister chased them up from the depths...

WHO'S AFRAID OF SEA SERPENTS?

Another creature that used to scare sailors stiff was the Sea Serpent. Around 20 or 30 meters long, it was said to attack ships and terrify crews. Sea Serpents do exist, but they are far shorter than the ones described by the sailors, usually only about 1 or 2 metres long.

SO WHAT WERE THOSE FAMED SEA SERPENTS?

WHAT WE KNOW:

There is a mean-faced fish, called the Giant Oarfish, which is silvery, scaleless and ribbon-shaped. Even though it can sometimes reach up to 17 metres in length, it is hard to believe that it could attack a ship! That's even before you consider that this fish is completely indifferent to humans: it usually lives somewhere between 300 and 1,000 metres beneath the sea!

Or we could return to our colossal squid: it may very well be that sailors thought the squid's tentacles, emerging from the water, were individual Sea Serpents attacking the ship.

DRAGON HUNTERS!

In every culture, there is a creature resembling a Dragon. It often appears as a symbol of life and power, a creative or protective spirit closer to a god than an actual animal. That's certainly true in the case of Huang Long in Chinese mythology, or Quetzalcoatl, the Aztecs' feathered serpent.

Commonly depicted with a snake's body, lizard's legs, eagle's talons, crocodile's jaws, lion's teeth and bat-like wings, the Dragon is a combination of several different animals. Amongst the Dragon's many portrayals is the Hydra of Greek mythology - a vicious sea monster with seven heads. Two of the most famous Hydras are the Lernaean Hydra, which was killed by Heracles, and Scylla, which was rumoured to live in the depths of the strait of Messina.

SO WHAT EXACTLY IS A DRAGON?

WHAT WE KNOW:

Amongst the most famous Dragon hunters is Saint George, a Christian soldier and the Patron Saint of England. According to the legend, Saint George saved a princess from certain death between a Dragon's jaws. After Saint George's legend became popular, tales of Dragon hunters spread like wildfire.

Originating from Libya in North Africa, the tale of Saint George's Dragon may well have referred to a crocodile. Most of the other famous dragons probably also started life as reptiles, even small ones like snakes, basilisks or monitor lizards. Take an ancestral fear of reptiles, add a pinch of ignorance and a spoonful of superstition, and all of a sudden, plain old reptiles get transformed into powerful magical monsters!

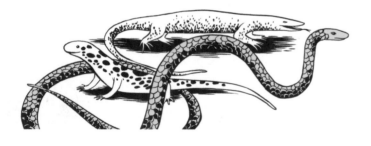

In the Middle Ages, the Dragon was said to have terrible powers and was accused of causing epidemics, fires, and famines. In Norse mythology, it spits fire and protects treasures. In the Christian tradition, it lives in a cave, from which one can hear its dreadful roar.

THE LOCH NESS MONSTER

This is undoubtedly the most famous monster of the 20th century. The legend telling of a monstrous creature living in a Scottish lake (or loch) starts to spread as early as 665 AD, but the modern myth only comes into existence in 1933 when the British newspaper The Daily Mail assigns the explorer Marmaduke Wetherell the mission of travelling to Loch Ness to verify the story. Even the newspaper didn't expect such an immediate and brilliant result: after only three days in Scotland, the explorer returned with pictures of the monster's footprints on the lake's beach.

The news immediately made the headlines: the Loch Ness Monster was real! But the euphoria didn't last long. London's Natural History Museum studied the photographs and concluded that they showed nothing but the footprints of a hippopotamus.

BUT HOW DID HIPPOS FIND THEIR WAY TO THE BEACH OF A SCOTTISH LAKE?

WHAT WE KNOW:

It's simple: stuffed hippopotamus feet were used as umbrella stands on the beaches of Loch Ness!

As you might imagine, everybody made fun of Marmaduke and his monster. But three months later the Daily Mail received a letter from the London-based surgeon Robert Wilson. It contained an old picture showing what looked like the head and neck of a dinosaur floating on the surface of the water!

Thanks to Wilson's photo, the myth of Nessie, a plesiosaur that survived the extinction of the dinosaurs and now swimming in the waters of Loch Ness persisted until 1994. It was only proved false when Marmaduke Wetherell's stepson confessed that Robert Wilson's picture was a fake! It actually showed a toy submarine with a long neck and fake dinosaur head attached. It was a trick Wetherell had planned all along to take revenge on everyone who had made fun of him!

But the legend endures and there are still many people today who remain convinced of the monster's existence and believe the photo is real.

Many witnesses have seen strange things in the lake. Numerous pictures and movies show these inexplicable phenomena. Some believe that the monster is simply a group of seals entering the lake through an underground passage. But this mysterious passage has never been found...

OGOPOGO AND HIS BROTHERS

Loch Ness isn't the only body of water thought to be haunted by monsters. Seas and lakes have always scared and mystified humans. Many witnesses believe that another plesiosaur called Ogopogo lives in the Okanagan Lake, in Canada. It has been spotted hundreds of times, and even filmed, and is said to be more than 13 metres long.
Similar dinosaurs are said to live in other lakes in Canada, the USA and other parts of the world. Another 14-metre long lizard is supposedly living in Lake Van, in Turkey. Many witnesses claim to have seen a creature that they call Selma in Lake Seljord, in Norway. And recently, unknown finned, seal-like creatures were filmed in Heaven Lake, on the border between China and North Korea!

SO WHAT COULD ALL THESE CREATURES BE?

WHAT WE KNOW:

All these creatures have common traits - witnesses describe them as having a dog head, a long neck, brown hair, a forked tail and snake-like movements. Others say they have an elongated head and scales on their backs.

It's possible that these mysterious creatures are just groups of eared seals, river dolphins (although they are increasingly rare nowadays, river dolphins used to be found in freshwater rivers and estuaries in many parts of the world, including China) or even sturgeons, which can grow up to 5 ½ metres in length and have large bony plates on their backs that look like the scales of a large reptile.

GUSTAVE, LAKE TANGANYIKA'S MONSTER

But it's hard to believe that an animal supposedly 12 metres long is in fact an eared seal - which is never more than 3 metres long. The size of these unknown creatures feeds their myths - monsters are always excessively large. Speaking of large, let's take a look at the gigantic case of Gustave.

A long time ago, in Lake Tanganyika, there was a legendary Nile Crocodile that, according to witnesses, was between 6 and 7 metres long – the largest ever recorded – almost twice the size of a common Nile Crocodile. People in the region called him Gustave and said that he had eaten at least 300 people in the course of his 60-year life. After trying many times to capture or film him, hunters killed Gustave in 2005.

BUT WHO REALLY WAS GUSTAVE?

WHAT WE KNOW:

Once measured, Gustave ended up just being a regular Nile Crocodile - he was only 4 metres long. Not actually that impressive for a Nile Croc, some members of this species measure up to 4.5 metres in length.

For curious readers:
Shortly after being killed, Gustave was actually served for dinner in the fancy restaurants of Bujumbura, the capital of Burundi!

BIGFOOT

In the North American forests of the early 19th century, a few witnesses claimed to have seen a mysterious creature covered in hair but walking like a man. In 1811, the mountain guide David Thompson found a 35-centimetre footprint in the snow!
Ever since, people have been talking about a gigantic creature that they nicknamed Bigfoot. But despite many sightings, no proof of Bigfoot's existence was found until 1967. At that time, while shooting a documentary in the Bluff Creek Valley, Roger Patterson and his friend Bob Gimlin spotted something like a big black gorilla walking through the trees around 30 metres away. The 20-second movie shot by the two friends is said to prove the existence of Bigfoot.

BUT IS THIS STORY TRUE? DOES BIGFOOT REALLY EXIST? IF HE DOES, WHAT KIND OF CREATURE COULD HE REALLY BE?

WHAT WE KNOW:

Some maintain that Bigfoot is a caveman that has survived until today; others say that it's just a gorilla... even though there are no gorillas in North America. And then again, some people think that it could be an unknown, ape-like hominid.

But there are those who think that the footprint found in the snow was fake, like all the ones found after it, and that the movie was just a practical joke by the two friends, one filming and the other dressed up as a great ape! Roger Patterson, for his part, maintained that his Bigfoot movie was authentic until the day he died.

The Yeti is another famously mysterious hominid. According to legends, he lives on Tibetan mountain summits. In 1954, the Daily Mail newspaper, which had sent Marmaduke Wetherell to confirm the existence of the Loch Ness monster, paid for a mission to Tibet to find traces of the Yeti, but all they discovered were large footprints on the snow that anybody could have faked.

Like Nessie, the Yeti has a multitude of cousins spread across the globe. Although they may go by different names, these mysterious hairy men are even said to haunt the mountains of Europe. Many legends and paintings depict the Wild Man of the Tyrol Mountains.

It's hard to say what these creatures really are. Perhaps they are just mountain hermits that time, superstition and the human taste for mystery have transformed into half-human half-beasts?

WARNING: STINKY MONSTER!

The case of the smelly Mapinguari, said to be living in the Amazon rainforest, is slightly different. It is described as a gigantic nocturnal animal that strolls through the jungle on four limbs. It has long arms and claws, the skin of a reptile and flaming red hair. It seems to avoid water. Maybe that's the reason it stinks so much... it never takes a bath!

WHAT COULD THE MAPINGUARI BE?

WHAT WE KNOW:

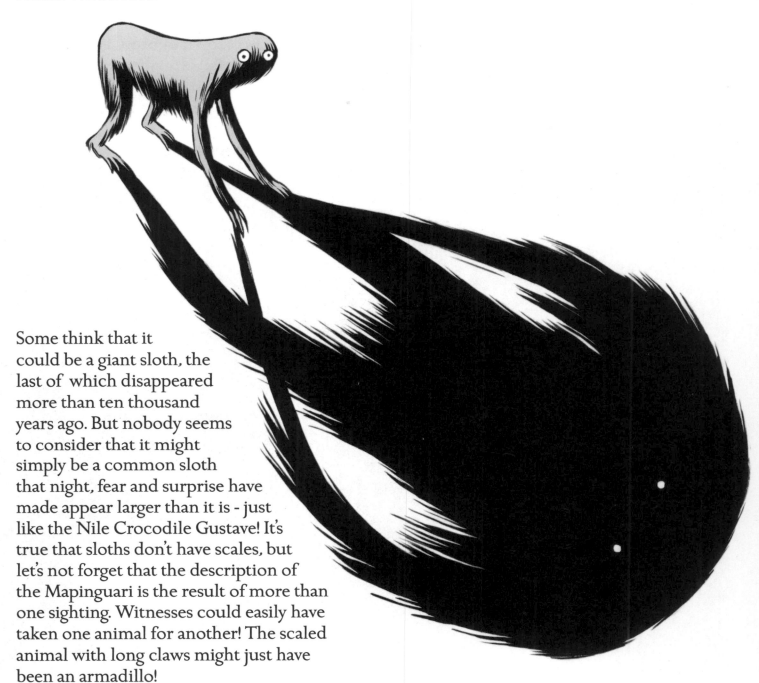

Some think that it could be a giant sloth, the last of which disappeared more than ten thousand years ago. But nobody seems to consider that it might simply be a common sloth that night, fear and surprise have made appear larger than it is - just like the Nile Crocodile Gustave! It's true that sloths don't have scales, but let's not forget that the description of the Mapinguari is the result of more than one sighting. Witnesses could easily have taken one animal for another! The scaled animal with long claws might just have been an armadillo!

THE COTTINGLEY FAIRIES

Frances and Elsie were 10 and 16 years old respectively when they borrowed Elsie's father's camera. While developing the photos, Elsie's father noticed creatures that looked like Fairies and, thinking that it was just a prank, he told the two girls off.. The story could easily have ended there, but two years later, Elsie's mother showed the picture to a large audience at a lecture about Fairies. The Fairies in the photo were named the Cottingley Fairies, after the place that the photo was taken.

The rumour that the two girls had managed to photograph Fairies soon reached the ears of Arthur Conan Doyle, the author of the Sherlock Holmes stories. Despite the advice of an expert in photography who insisted the pictures were faked, Conan Doyle published an article claiming the Fairies were real. Encouraged by the attention, the girls continued to take pictures and Conan Doyle continued to believe them, even winning the support of Harold Snelling, the foremost photography expert of the time.

In 1976, almost sixty years after the first photo, the two cousins still maintained that the pictures were real. It was only in 1981 that Frances admitted that four out of the five pictures were faked. The following year, Elsie confirmed the story.

BUT WHAT ABOUT THE FIFTH PICTURE?

WHAT WE KNOW:

Frances and Elsie's Fairies were actually cardboard cutouts from a children's book. But people who want to believe in fairies have always rejected this explanation because nobody has ever found the book that the girls used.

If it sounds strange that Arthur Conan Doyle would have been so naive about Fairies, keep in mind that, far from sharing the rational mindset of his famous character Sherlock Holmes, Conan Doyle was a great believer in supernatural creatures and spiritualism. It just goes to show, given half a chance, people will believe whatever they want to believe.

ROALD DAHL'S GREMLINS

Arthur Conan Doyle wasn't the only famous 20th century author to acknowledge the existence of supernatural beings. In 1942, when he was a pilot in the Royal Air Force, Roald Dahl - not yet the famous children's author that we all know and love - was flying a B-25 Mitchell bomber.

After a malfunction forced Dahl to land, he decided it was high time to inform the public of a problem that had been troubling the Royal Air Force for months: Gremlins.

A rumour had spread among RAF pilots that mysterious breakdowns were being caused by Gremlins: small and mischievous creatures from Irish folklore.

SO WHAT WERE THESE TINY CREATURES?

WHAT WE KNOW:

The breakdowns can be easily explained in a rational, scientific way. During the Second World War, planes were put together in a hurry. They were rushed to be available as soon as possible so they probably weren't really ready for flight.

A few of the incidents were almost certainly linked to magnetic malfunctions. Unlike the old wooden Hurricanes, the new Spitfires were the first fighters made entirely out of metal. The metal interfered with magnetic instruments, causing dangerous malfunctions that sometimes led to accidents.

But despite this evidence the RAF pilots - Roald Dahl amongst them - preferred to believe that these accidents were caused by strange creatures that nobody had ever seen. Go figure...

MY NAME IS JENNY HANIVER

The ease with which people accept the most improbable myths has, from the beginning of time, inspired forgers to fabricate objects that apparently prove the existence of legendary creatures. Forgers created fakes for plenty of reasons: to try and make some money, to become famous, or just to have a laugh.

The Jenny Haniver is a classic example of a fake creature invented by men. It is a ray or a skate fish that has been dried out and made to look human. If you take a look at the belly of this fish, with its white skin, big mouth and gills like threatening eyes... you'll see it's actually pretty terrifying!

The Jenny Haniver has been sold at markets from Germany to England since the 16th century.

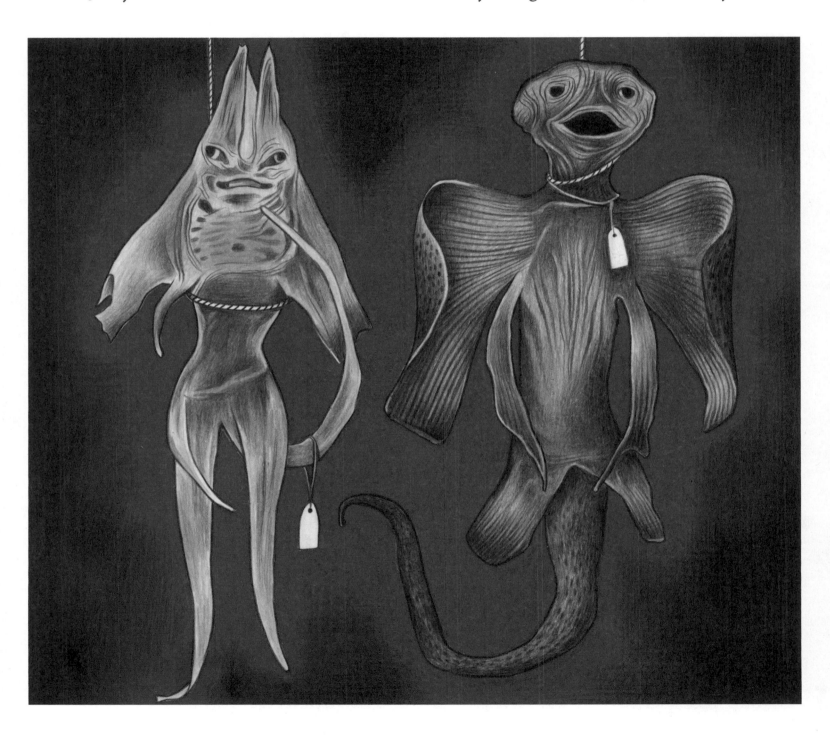

BUT WHERE COULD YOU FIND JENNY HANIVER TODAY?

WHAT WE KNOW:

The Internet is awash with supposed alien mummies that you can buy for a mere $75! The culprit: who else but Jenny Haniver?!

In 19th century Japan, forgers specialised in making fake Mermaids. They created mummies of these legendary creatures by carefully sewing the top half of an embalmed monkey to the bottom half of a dried fish, calling the beast a Ningyo.

Nowadays, the American sculptor Juan Cabana uses a similar technique to build fake Mermaids in his studio in Florida. His creations are sold to art collectors and pictures of his works are exhibited on his website. But people can't help themselves – they still use Cabana's pictures to invent stories of Mermaids found on beaches. And so the myth lives on!

LYING LUMBERJACKS

While some people faked footprints or shaped animal bodies into mermaid mummies, others just created brand new legends out of thin air!
The Fearsome Critters were monsters made up by lumberjacks in North America to frighten and make fun of newcomers. Between the end of the 18th and the beginning of the 19th centuries, stories of the Fearsome Critters spread through the continent's forests. The strange bestiary created by these inventive lumberjacks stretched to at least 80 animals.

WOULD YOU LIKE TO MEET SOME OF THEM?

THE AXEHANDLE HOUND
A bloodhound whose diet consists exclusively of the handles of axes.

THE FLITTERBICK
A flying squirrel that can kill a bull by punching it between the eyes.

THE GILLYGALOO
A bird that makes its nest on the top of a mountain and lays eggs that are square, so they don't roll over.

THE PINNACLE GOOSE
A bird with only one wing, which can only fly around in circles.

THE GOOFANG
A fish that swims backwards to keep water out of its eyes.

THE SPLINTERCAT
A cat that uses its stiff forehead to smash into trees and find the delicious, sweet sap that it loves.

THE CACTUS CAT
A cat with hair-like thorns that lives in the desert and likes to get drunk on cactus water.

THE HOOP SNAKE
When in danger, this snake bites its tail, curls up like a wheel and speeds away.

THE UPLAND TROUT
A fish that lives up a tree and never touches the water. The lumberjacks used to send newcomers to hunt it for dinner!

BEWARE OF THE FULL MOON!

Few modern movie monsters are better known than the Werewolf (also called the Lycanthrope) a human being who transforms into a wolf-man on the night of the full moon. According to legend, the bite of the Werewolf spreads the curse and the creature can only be harmed with silver weapons!

Just like Sea Serpents or Wild Men, Werewolves appear in every culture. In Greek mythology, King Lycaon offended Zeus and was transformed into a half-man, half-wolf creature as a punishment.

In the past, people who were suspected of being a Werewolf were burnt alive, just like witches. In France, 'Werewolves' were sent to the stake up until the 17th century!

DID WEREWOLVES REALLY EXIST?

WHAT WE KNOW:

It's easy to believe that the myth of the Lycanthrope was born of an ancestral fear of wolves, but men who looked almost exactly like wolves really did exist. They had hypertrichosis, a disease provoking excessive hair growth on the body and face. Fedor Jeftichew was a famous sideshow performer with hypertrichosis. He used to tour with circuses all around Europe before being brought to the United States by P.T. Barnum, a man known for having made a fortune out of strange-looking people like Fedor.

KEEP THOSE TEETH AWAY FROM MY NECK!

The word Vampire comes from the Serbian word *vampir*. The blood-drinking monster can be found across the globe, going by a different name in each location:
Vrykolakas in Greece, Penanggalan in Malaysia, and Kukudhi in Albania.
But the most famous Vampire is, of course, Dracula. The blood-sucking count has starred in many movies, and is known for his particular taste for young women's blood. The name Dracula comes from the Romanian word *dracul*, which means "the dragon".

SO WHAT'S THE LINK BETWEEN VAMPIRES AND ROMANIA?

WHAT WE KNOW:

The Dracula that we've all seen on the silver screen was inspired by a historical figure who really existed. A Romanian prince called Vlad Tapes, was known for the grisly practice of impaling his enemies. With time, the myth of this famously bloody prince took on a new dimension and Vlad became a blood drinker.

The tale of the bloodthirsty count was truly cemented in people's imaginations by Bram Stoker's novel Dracula. Since then, Vampires have become the stars of countless movies, novels and comics. Now everybody knows that being bitten by a Vampire can pass on the curse, that Vampires don't cast a shadow and that they have no reflection. But most importantly, they can't stand garlic. To repel a Vampire, you should always wear garlic around your neck... that is, if you don't mind running the risk of repelling fellow humans too!

To kill a Vampire, you have to expose it to direct sunlight or pierce its heart with a stake made of maple or ash wood. Good luck getting close enough to one without falling victim to its sharp fangs and appetite for blood!

WITCH-HUNT

Since the dawn of time, women have been associated with the legendary image of the Witch, creatures gifted with supernatural powers and the ability to concoct evil potions and spells. The Inquisition, established by the Catholic Church in the fifteenth century to punish heretics, used torture to extract confessions from innocent women. Witchcraft soon came to be considered an act of heresy.

Courts tried and brutalised hundreds of people accused of witchcraft all over Europe and the newly discovered Americas until the Inquisition was finally abolished in the early nineteenth century. One of the most terrifying chapters in witch-hunt history was the Salem Witch Trials. In 1691, in a small American village, two young girls started foaming at the mouth and acting like they were mad. Doctors, unable to say what was wrong, decided the cause was witchcraft. A slave called Tituba was arrested and during her trial confessed to having practiced witchcraft. She was hung. Other villagers pleaded guilty or accused their neighbours to try and save themselves. Before the trial was over, twenty people, including children, were arrested, tried and hung.

WHAT REALLY HAPPENED IN SALEM?

WHAT WE KNOW:

Experts believe that poison was at the root of the mass hysteria that struck the village of Salem. At the time in North America, a grain called rye was a crucial part of people's diet, essential to the making of bread.

But rye is often attacked by a fungus called ergot. The infection caused by infected rye is called ergotism.

Ergotism causes serious nervous issues, hallucinations and sometimes even death. It's very likely that Salem's madness was caused by ergot. The fungus, which can resist high temperatures, had survived in the town's bread supply.

People point out that when the year's crop of rye ran out, both the hallucinations and the witchy convulsions ceased, placing the blame squarely on the fungus Ergot.

ZOMBIES - THE WALKING DEAD

Zombies, or Walking Dead, are also regular actors in horror movies. A radioactive leak or an earthquake, and bam! Corpses jump out of their graves to eat people! Yum!
But Zombie stories, like Werewolf stories or Vampire stories, have their roots in reality. Well, almost...
In Haïti people practice a religion called Voodoo that holds magic and superstition in high regard. It is thought that a Bokor - a Voodoo sorcerer - can steal someone's soul, wake him or her from death and turn them into a slave – a Zombie.

BUT DO THEY REALLY EXIST?

WHAT WE KNOW:

A study conducted during the 1980s found that the Bokor probably controlled people using a neurotoxin created from the poison of the fugu, a type of pufferfish. The neurotoxin causes a state of apparent death and the supposed complete obedience of the "exhumed corpse".
In reality, Zombies are just drugged slaves forced to work in sugar plantations. Obedient workers that never go on strike!

THE MYSTERY OF THE MOKELE-MBEMBE

800 kilometres north of Brazzaville, the capital of the Republic of the Congo, is a vast, swampy area where rumours tell of a frightening creature - the Mokele-mbembe. Described for the first time by a French missionary in the 18th century, he claimed the Mokele-mbembe was as big as an elephant, with a small snake-like head, a 2 to 3 metre long neck, hippopotamus feet and a crocodile tail.

WHAT ANIMAL COULD LURK BENEATH THIS MYSTERY?

WHAT WE KNOW:

This description sounds remarkably similar to the Sauropods, a group of animals that disappeared 65.5 million years ago! From 1913 onwards, expeditions set out in search of the Mokele-mbembe. But they returned with little more than a few pictures and some vague footage. According to some theories the Mokele-mbembe might be an unknown species of monitor lizard.
Others say that it's a softshell turtle whose long neck, small head and aggressive attitude match the descriptions of the monster.

The softshell turtle isn't as big as the legendary Mokele-mbembe but sceptics still argue that it is possible that Pygmies, terrified of an animal that they didn't know, got the measurements wrong. They claim that this situation is far more likely to be the case than that a dinosaur is living quietly in Africa without anybody ever having taken its picture.
Still, the Congolese rainforests are some of the least explored territories on Earth - you never know what may be hiding in their thick forests...

THE COELACANTH'S RETURN

In his book, published in 1932, the explorer Frank M. Welland claimed that on a trip
to Zambia he spotted a strange flying animal. The locals called the creature Kongamato.
Welland described it as a featherless bird with a wingspan of up to 2 metres, reddish
or black skin and a long sharp beak. It looked exactly like a Pterosaur, a flying reptile
that disappeared millions of years ago.
Apparently these animals have even been sighted in Texas.
Here we go again - yet another long-lost dinosaur making a comeback!

WHY IS EVERYONE SEEING DINOSAURS?

WHAT WE KNOW:

Let's see. If so many people believe that animals we thought had gone extinct million of years ago are still alive today, that's because it's happened at least once before.

Towards the end of 1938, near the coast of South Africa, some fishermen accidentally caught a Coelacanth – A REAL ONE – but it was far from being airborne. The Coelacanth is a fish that everybody thought had gone extinct millions of years ago! Other specimens captured afterwards brought the confirmation of this astonishing news: the Coelacanth is still around! But it's a fish, not a Pterosaur.

The sea is full of mysteries and may still conceal many species that we never expected to see, except as fossils.
So beware! In early 2007, Japanese fishermen noticed a strange shark, a fish that really seemed prehistoric.

The piece of news zoomed around the world and a team of marine scientists called to the spot may have filmed a species that was believed to have gone extinct 80 million years ago!
But soon after, this specimen was identified as a frilled shark, a lesser-known species of shark. Its enormous head and eel body had convinced people of its prehistoric origins.

So still no Pterosaur but a Coelacanth's not too bad.

THE CHUPACABRA CONUNDRUM

One of the most recent legends is the tale of the Chupacabra - a creature that preys on chickens and goats. That's probably where it got its name - Chupacabra is Spanish for "goat sucker". Sighted mostly in Latin America and Florida, it is said to look like a hairless kangaroo with the head of a dog. It behaves like a vampire coyote, literally sucking the blood from its prey, leaving behind corpses that have been bled-dry.

It's also said to possess the ability to change colour, as well as other supernatural powers, such as hypnosis and telepathy. Some say it is the result of genetic experiments, while others think the Chupacabra may have come from outer space!

SO WHAT HIDES BEHIND THIS MYSTERY?

WHAT WE KNOW:

The videos of the Chupacabra, often blurry and hard to follow, and the pictures, usually faked, don't help much with identifying the creature.
But if you trust the descriptions, the Chupacabra looks a lot like a rare species of Mexican hairless dog called the Xoloitzcuintle.

DNA tests on dead specimens have proven that it is an ordinary dog with nothing extraterrestrial about it at all!

EPILOGUE

If you read this far then you've learned the truth - monsters really do exist!
They're just not magical or supernatural creatures. In most cases, they're simply strange
or scary animals that had never been seen before. Fear has the power to transform the
unknown into something far bigger and more dangerous than it really is!

So, if mermaids, vampires and dinosaurs don't exist, can we still believe in mysteries?

The answer is... YES.

Just because this book intended to show that the magical creatures in ancient legends
are really just normal animals, it doesn't mean that there is nothing left to discover. Deep
in the rainforests or buried under the polar ice caps, at the bottom of the sea or at the
centre of the Earth, there must still be plenty of monsters out there...

So, what are you waiting for?

Go find them!

NOTES

Sloth - Toothless mammal.

Heretic - In the 15th century the Catholic Church treated many people who had different opinions than themselves as heretics and would violently persecute them.

Hominid - Family of primates, from the first great apes to the humans.

Plesiosaur - From the Latin *plesios* which means 'close to' and *sauros* which means 'lizard'. The plesiosaur was a great sea reptile that could be up to 10 metres long.